Cornerstones of Freedom

Asian-Americans in the Old West

GAIL SAKURAI

CHILDREN'S PRESS®
A Division of Grolier Publishing
New York • London • Hong Kong • Sydney
Danbury, Connecticut

Visit Children's Press on the Internet at:
http://publishing.grolier.com

Library of Congress Cataloging-in-Publication Data

Sakurai, Gail.
  Asian-Americans in the old West / Gail Sakurai.
    p. cm.— (Cornerstones of freedom)
  Includes index.
  Summary: Describes the important role of the Chinese, Japanese, and other
Asians in the settlement of the American West.
  ISBN: 0-516-21152-8 (lib. bdg.)   0-516-27035-4 (pbk.)
1. Asian Americans—West (U.S.)—History Juvenile literature. 2. West (U.S.)—
History Juvenile literature. 3. West (U.S.)—Ethnic relations Juvenile literature.
[1. Asian Americans—West (U.S.)—History. 2. West (U.S.)—History. 3. Race
relations.] I. Title. II. Series.
F596.3.06S35   2000
978`.00495073—dc21
                                                    99-24463
                                                    CIP

©2000 Children's Press®
A Division of Grolier Publishing Co., Inc.
All rights reserved. Published simultaneously in Canada.
Printed in the United States of America.
1 2 3 4 5 6 7 8 9 10 R 09 08 07 06 05 04 03 02 01 00

GROLIER
PUBLISHING

"Gold! Gold! They've discovered gold!" The excited cry echoed across the land. On January 24, 1848, a sawmill worker named James Marshall found gold at Sutter's Mill, near present-day Sacramento, California. News of the discovery soon reached San Francisco. From there, "gold fever," the intense desire to find gold, spread rapidly. The fever was fueled by wild tales of streams paved with glittering yellow flakes and ground covered with shining golden nuggets. According to the stories, the precious metal was just waiting for some lucky people to wander along and gather it up.

James Marshall stands beside Sutter's Mill, the site where he discovered gold on January 24, 1848.

Throughout California, men quit their jobs to go hunt for gold. One observer of the Gold Rush wrote, "the blacksmith dropped his hammer . . . the farmer his sickle, the baker his loaf . . ." and ran off to the mines. Hundreds of mining camps sprang up overnight in the foothills of the Sierra Nevada mountains. Fewer than one hundred people were left in San Francisco, usually a town of more than one thousand.

Before long, reports of the California gold strike had spread across the United States. Thousands of people became infected with gold fever. They left their families, homes, and jobs to seek their fortunes in the mines. In just a few months, word of the California Gold Rush had

When news of the discovery of gold spread throughout the United States and the world, thousands of men rushed to California in search of a fortune.

spread across the world to Europe, Australia, and even China. Upon learning the news, the Chinese nicknamed California *Gum Saan*, the land of the "Golden Mountains." Exaggerated stories and advertisements encouraged the Chinese to come to America. One enticing ad claimed: "Americans are very rich people. They

This traveler's guide to California contained information and maps for gold miners headed to the region.

want the Chinaman to come and will make him very welcome. There you will have great pay, large houses, and food and clothing of the finest description." For many poor farmers, the lure of gold was impossible to resist. Faced with high taxes, crop failures, and other hardships at home, thousands of young men decided to seek their fortunes in the land of the Golden Mountains. They left their wives and families behind, intending to be gone only a few years at most, before striking it rich and returning to China as wealthy men.

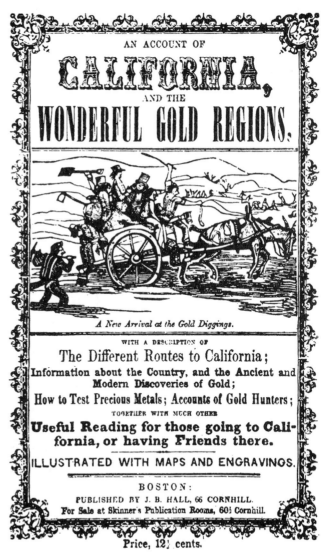

AN ACCOUNT OF

CALIFORNIA,

AND THE

WONDERFUL GOLD REGIONS.

A New Arrival at the Gold Diggings.

WITH A DESCRIPTION OF

The Different Routes to California;

Information about the Country, and the Ancient and Modern Discoveries of Gold;

How to Test Precious Metals; Accounts of Gold Hunters;

TOGETHER WITH MUCH OTHER

Useful Reading for those going to California, or having Friends there.

ILLUSTRATED WITH MAPS AND ENGRAVINGS.

BOSTON:
PUBLISHED BY J. B. HALL, 66 CORNHILL.
For Sale at Skinner's Publication Rooms, 60½ Cornhill.

Price, 12½ cents.

Their first hurdle was to obtain enough money for the passage to California. The fare was about $40. Most Chinese farmers earned only $20 to $30 a year. A few men received loans and gifts of money from family and friends, but most had to borrow from professional moneylenders at high repayment rates. Others entered into labor contracts with employers in the United States. Under this system the employer paid the fare, and in return the traveler agreed to work for a specific number of years at little or no pay.

During the long, difficult voyage across the Pacific Ocean from Asia, passengers were confined to stuffy, overcrowded compartments below decks. When the ship finally docked in San Francisco, the travelers caught their first

Chinese immigrants to the United States endured long, uncomfortable voyages across the Pacific Ocean.

breath of fresh air and glimpse of land in weeks. As the Chinese men gazed eagerly at the land of the Golden Mountains, a number of startling sights greeted them. San Francisco Bay was filled with dozens of

Chinese immigrants arrive in San Francisco to be approved for entry into the United States.

abandoned ships, for no sooner did a ship arrive than its crew deserted to search for gold. The sprawling city swarmed with people who spoke English, a language that was unfamiliar to the Chinese. To the Chinese, these Americans seemed very strange.

Since most Americans at that time had never seen an Asian before, the Chinese men looked equally odd to the Americans. The newcomers had golden-brown skin and narrow eyes, and their long black hair hung in a single braid down the middle of their backs. They wore loose coats and pants of blue cotton. Bundles of possessions dangled from long bamboo poles that rested across their shoulders. Everything about their appearance set the Chinese apart as strangers in a strange land.

The new arrivals from China didn't speak English and were not familiar with American customs. Because they considered themselves sojourners, or temporary residents who would eventually return to their own country, they made little attempt to learn American ways. They tended to stick together for moral support and formed their own Chinese communities in the land of the Golden Mountains. The area of San Francisco where many Chinese lived became known as "Chinatown." That colorful, bustling neighborhood was filled with sidewalk vegetable stands, small shops, and restaurants. Chinatown was a home away from home where the new migrants could enjoy the sights of familiar faces, the sounds of their native language, and the smells and tastes of favorite Chinese foods.

A view of San Francisco's Chinatown during the 1850s

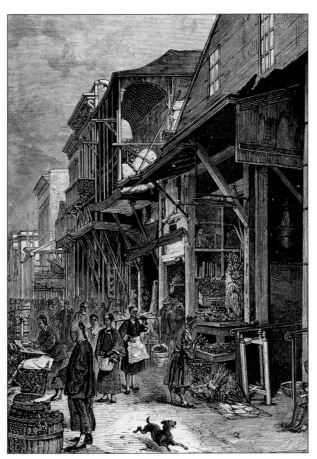

The Chinese residents of San Francisco soon formed mutual aid societies to welcome newcomers and help them get settled. These organizations were usually based on family or regional ties. Eventually, the various associations merged into the Chinese Six Companies, one company for each of the main districts in China that the migrants came from. The Six Companies looked after the well-being of their people in California. They also made sure that the sojourners repaid their debts before returning to their homeland.

Many mining camps had their own small Chinatowns. Chinese gold miners worked in groups, sharing the backbreaking labor as well as any earnings. They usually mined old, deserted sites that other miners had abandoned. Although the Asians posed little threat to American livelihood, some Americans began to resent the large number of Chinese who immigrated to California. When the first gold was found at Sutter's Mill in 1848, there were only seven Chinese in all of California. By 1852, nearly twenty-five thousand Chinese had settled in California.

Chinese gold miners split the profits from the sites where they found gold.

Americans decided to stop this Chinese "invasion." In 1852, they persuaded the California legislature to impose a special license tax of $3 a month on foreign miners. The purpose of this tax was to reduce the number of Asians coming to California and to discourage them from mining for gold.

Eventually, as the California gold mines dried up, some Chinese migrants moved east to the lands that would later become the states of Idaho, Montana, and Nevada to look for new mining opportunities. Many sojourners gave up mining altogether and went into different lines of work. Some found jobs in factories, while others took positions as servants in wealthy homes. A number became merchants or opened their own small businesses. The laundry business was especially favored because it didn't require much money or equipment to

The lack of women in the West to do traditional "women's work" made laundry services a booming business. As a result, many Chinese who established laundry businesses prospered.

A Chinese farmer tends an irrigation ditch in a California orchard.

get started, and there was a great demand for laundry services in the American West.

Another popular occupation among the Chinese was farming. Many migrants had been farmers back home, and they were experts at coaxing crops from small patches of soil. They were also skilled at reclaiming swamps and marshes. In California, Chinese workers dug hundreds of drainage ditches and constructed miles of levees and dikes. This turned thousands of acres of marshland into rich farmland suitable for fruit orchards and vegetable gardens. Fruits and vegetables became important crops in California, Oregon, and Washington Territory. In Oregon, Chinese immigrant Ah Bing made a lasting contribution to American agriculture when he developed the famous Bing cherry in 1875.

Some Chinese grew tired of working as laborers on large American-owned farms. They preferred to grow crops on their own plots of land. Since Chinese were not allowed to own property, they entered into tenant farmer agreements with American landowners. Under such an arrangement, the tenant farmer was given the use of the land and farming equipment, and in exchange the landowner received a share of the profits.

In the 1860s, Chinese workers received an opportunity for employment in railroad construction. The United States government decided to extend the railroad lines across the continent to link the western states with the major American cities in the east. The government granted contracts to two companies, the Union Pacific Railroad and the Central Pacific Railroad. The Union Pacific started laying tracks at Omaha,

Many Chinese had to be content with working as tenant farmers because they were not allowed to own land.

Nebraska, and built westward, while the Central Pacific began construction in Sacramento, California, and built eastward.

The Central Pacific Railroad hired fifty Chinese laborers on a trial basis. The company quickly discovered that the Asians were hard working, honest, and dependable. Company president Leland Stanford praised the workmen as "quiet, peaceable, industrious, economical—ready and apt to learn all the different kinds of work" involved in railroad building. They not only laid tracks, they also cleared trees, blasted rock, shoveled dirt, and drove supply wagons.

Leland Stanford

The railroad employed as many Chinese as it could find, and even sent agents to China to hire more laborers. Altogether, more than ten thousand Chinese migrants worked on the Central Pacific Railroad between 1864 and 1869. Construction crews pushed the train tracks through the wilderness. They battled blizzards and snowdrifts 30 to 40 feet (9 to 12 meters) deep as they struggled to cross the rugged Sierra Nevada mountains. They tunneled through jagged mountain peaks and built bridges across steep canyons.

Finally, in May 1869, the Union Pacific's westward track and the Central Pacific's eastward track met at Promontory Summit, Utah, in the desert north of Great Salt Lake. On the morning of May 10, a crowd of 1,500 people gathered for the official ceremony joining the two railways. The occasion marked the completion of the world's first transcontinental railroad, a rail system that linked the United States from coast to coast. The Central Pacific portion of the railroad, running from Sacramento to Promontory Summit, was almost entirely a Chinese accomplishment.

Nearly half of the Chinese men who came to the United States eventually returned to China. Of those who stayed, only a few could afford to have their families join them. Chin Gee-Hee was one of the fortunate settlers. He came to the United States in 1862, at the age of eighteen. He took a job at a lumber mill in Washington Territory, and in a few years he saved enough money to send for his wife. Chin's wife joined him and worked as a cook at the lumber mill. In 1875, their son, Chin Lem, was the first ethnic Chinese child born in Washington.

This photograph is a typical view of a Washington lumber mill in the late 1800s.

The rest of the Chinese immigrants stayed in the United States out of necessity. They didn't have enough money to send for their wives and children, nor were they able to pay for their own fares back to China. Their earnings barely stretched far enough to feed themselves, repay their ticket debts, and send a little money home to their families.

Representatives from the Chinese Six Companies explained this situation in a speech to the U.S. Congress in 1876: "Expensive rents, expensive living. A day without work means a day without food. For this reason, though wages are [high], yet they are compelled to labor and live in poverty, quite unable to return to their native land."

Many Chinese who didn't earn enough money to return to China lived in "neighborhoods" of run-down homes.

Those Chinese who decided to live permanently in the United States rarely felt completely at home. Differences in language, customs, religion, and appearance set them apart from other American residents. In addition, Chinese were not allowed to become citizens. The United States Naturalization Law of 1790 restricted American citizenship to white people. After the Civil War (1861–65), the Fourteenth Amendment to the Constitution gave citizenship rights to former slaves. But Asians were excluded from American citizenship.

The differences in appearance, clothing, and customs between Chinese and Americans kept Chinese immigrant families such as this one from feeling that they would ever fit in to U.S. society.

By 1870, there were 63,000 Chinese in the United States, most of them in California and other western states. At the same time that the Chinese were settling in the American West, millions of immigrants from Ireland, Germany, and other European countries were coming to the east coast of the United States. A number of Americans became alarmed by the flood of foreigners. They feared that the newcomers would take jobs away from Americans.

Then, during the 1870s, the United States entered an economic depression. Many businesses failed and thousands of people lost their jobs. Foreigners, especially the Chinese, made easy targets for hostility and resentment. European immigrants could blend into American society once they had learned English and adopted American customs. Asians, however, because of their distinct appearance, stood out. Racial and religious prejudice also played a part in the negative feelings directed at the Chinese.

While Chinese immigrants poured into the American West, the East was serving as a gateway to the United States for millions of European immigrants, who arrived at Ellis Island, in New York Harbor.

As the economic hard times continued, anti-Asian feelings grew. American labor unions pressed for the removal of the Chinese and adopted the slogan, "The Chinese Must Go!" In 1877, anti-Chinese riots erupted in San Francisco and spread throughout California. A San Francisco newspaper reported: "It is scarcely safe for a Chinaman to walk the streets in certain parts of this city. When seen, whether by day or night, they are mercilessly pelted with stones."

As Americans became increasingly resentful of the number of Asian immigrants, anti-Chinese rallies, such as this one in San Francisco in 1877, became more common.

Finally, the U.S. Congress reacted to public pressure and passed the Chinese Exclusion Act of 1882, which prohibited all Chinese laborers from entering the United States. Chinese men still in the United States were no longer allowed to bring their families from China. As there were few Chinese women in the United States at that time, unmarried men had little chance of finding a Chinese wife. They would have to return to

This photograph of a young, married Chinese couple was taken in 1884. The Chinese Exclusion Act, however, made photos like this one rare because it became more difficult for Chinese men to find Chinese women to marry.

China if they wished to marry. As a result of the Exclusion Act, Chinese immigration dropped dramatically from a high of 39,500 people in 1882 to just ten people in 1887.

American businesses that depended on Chinese workers soon found themselves facing a severe labor shortage. To fill the gap, business owners turned to Japan, a brand new source of labor. For more than two hundred years, Japan had been closed to the outside world, and the Japanese were forbidden from visiting foreign lands. Then, in the late 1880s, the emperor of Japan lifted the travel ban, and thousands of eager Japanese workers went to the United States.

This new state of affairs was the result of the trade agreement that Commodore Matthew C. Perry of the United States Navy negotiated with Japan thirty years earlier. On July 8, 1853, Perry sailed into Tokyo Bay with a message for the Japanese emperor from United States president Franklin Pierce. The United States wished to establish trade between the two countries because American merchants wanted a new market for their goods. As a token of friendship, Perry brought gifts of modern, American-made guns and machinery. The Japanese were impressed with the weapons and equipment. They realized that they would need to produce similar goods in order to compete as a trading nation and to protect themselves against foreign invaders.

Commodore Matthew C. Perry (top) and President Franklin Pierce (bottom)

Factories, such as this one where silk was made, were just one of many improvements the Japanese made to modernize their society.

The Japanese quickly began a major program of modernization. They started building factories and improving their military forces. Education was required for both boys and girls, and women were encouraged to take jobs alongside men in factories. In just a few years, the Japanese transformed their country from an agricultural society into a modern, industrialized world power. However, in order to pay the costs of the industrial and military buildups, the government set high land taxes. Many poor farmers could not afford to pay the taxes and, as a result, lost their farms. When the government began to allow foreign travel, these farmers jumped at the chance to go to the United States, where wages were high. They intended to work hard, make a fortune, return home, and buy back the lands they had lost.

The Japanese emperor was aware of the difficulties that the Chinese had encountered in the United States, and he wanted his citizens to avoid similar problems. Therefore, the Japanese government looked after the welfare of its citizens living in other countries. Japan also wanted to preserve its national honor and fine reputation. The Japanese government gave travel permits only to those who were educated, healthy, strong, and of good moral character.

Like the Chinese who came to the United States before them, the Japanese at first considered themselves sojourners. They planned eventually to return to their own country. Unlike the Chinese, however, many of the Japanese men brought their wives with them. These Japanese couples often began having children and putting down roots in America. Children who were born in the United States were automatically American citizens, even though the parents weren't allowed to become citizens. As time went on, Japanese immigrants began to think of themselves as settlers rather than sojourners.

Japanese immigrants, including these California farmworkers, often had their families with them. This made it easier for them to remain in the United States.

Japanese newcomers settled on the west coast of the United States, particularly in California, but also in Washington and Oregon. They joined fishing crews, worked in lumber mills, and toiled in factories. Some Japanese moved to Utah, Wyoming, and Colorado to work on railroads or to take jobs in mines. A number of Japanese immigrants opened small businesses, stores, and restaurants. However, most worked as farm laborers in California. Before long, these farmworkers grew tired of picking fruit for American landowners. They wanted to farm their own land. Within a few years, the Japanese became successful farmers. They turned vast areas of swampland into farmland. Soon they were producing most of California's strawberries, peppers, celery, tomatoes, and other fruits and vegetables. The Japanese also were the first to grow rice successfully in California.

The Japanese immigrants' success aroused the anger and fear of many American

Small Japanese-owned stores such as this one were established wherever Japanese immigrants settled.

farmers. They worried that the Japanese would put them out of business. As had happened with the Chinese, anti-Japanese feelings grew. Americans started demanding that the U.S. government put an end to Japanese immigration. Faced with resentment from Americans, Japanese immigrants formed their own trade unions and social groups. They also found protection and mutual support in Japanese communities such as "Little Tokyo," the Japanese area of Los Angeles. In spite of the difficulties encountered, Japanese immigration continued. By 1900, there were nearly 72,000 Japanese living in the United States.

Japanese farmers tend a rice field in northern California.

A few Japanese-Americans, such as farmer George Shima, defied anti-Japanese hostility. Shima arrived in California in 1887 and took a job as a potato picker. He was ambitious and soon became a farmer. Shima specialized in growing potatoes. By 1912, he controlled 10,000 acres (4,047 hectares) of potatoes valued at $500,000. He became known as the "Potato King." In spite of his wealth and success, when he bought a house in a fashionable area of Berkeley, California, his American neighbors tried to drive him out. They didn't want a Japanese family living in their neighborhood. But Shima refused to move. When he died in 1926, he was worth $15 million and had become well known and respected throughout the San Francisco Bay Area.

However, American hostility against Japanese settlers did not stop. No matter how carefully the Japanese government selected people to go to the United States, it was nearly impossible to prevent Americans from resenting the immigrants. When California and other western states started passing laws that discriminated against Japanese immigrants, Japan registered an official complaint with the United States government in Washington, D.C. President Theodore Roosevelt wanted to maintain good relations with Japan, and he tried to avoid offending the Japanese. At the same time, Roosevelt had to consider the feelings of Americans who wanted to halt Japanese immigration to the United States.

Finally, in 1908, Roosevelt negotiated the Gentlemen's Agreement with Japan. According to the agreement, Japan would stop sending its citizens to the United States. In return, the United States would not pass laws that discriminated against Japanese immigrants. A special provision allowed Japanese already in the United States to bring their family members, including parents, spouses, and children, to join them. Although the Gentlemen's Agreement was designed to halt Japanese immigration, it had the opposite effect, as a result of the family provision. Japanese-Americans took advantage of it and brought their families to the United States in huge numbers. Japanese immigration more than doubled in the years following the agreement, and Japanese-American families and communities continued to grow.

President Theodore Roosevelt (left) and Japanese Emperor Mutsuhito (right) signed the Gentleman's Agreement, which was designed to stop Japanese immigration to the United States.

The 1900s brought increased industrialization and a more urban way of life to the American West. The days of the Old West frontier were over. However, Asian immigration did not end. People from Korea, the Philippines, and India began moving to the United States in the early 1900s. Although each of these groups had its own distinct culture, language, and customs, their treatment followed the same pattern as the Chinese and the Japanese who had arrived earlier. Americans feared that the newcomers would take away their jobs. Protests and sometimes violence followed, and then laws were passed to discourage and prevent the Asians from coming to the United States. Finally, the United States government passed the Immigration Act of 1924, which prohibited the entry of all Asians.

Restrictive immigration laws designed to prevent foreigners—especially Asians—from moving to the United States continued until 1952. The Immigration and Nationality Act of 1952 reopened Asian immigration in a limited way. It also gave Asians the right to become American citizens. In 1965, immigration quotas based on race and ethnic origin ended.

The taming of the frontier and the development of the American West would not have been possible without the contributions of Asian-Americans. They are currently the fastest-growing minority group in the United States. The U.S. Census

Bureau estimates that in 2000, Asian-Americans will number about ten million people. Today, Asian-Americans are prominent in virtually every field, including literature, the arts, science, medicine, politics, and sports. This talented, accomplished, and diverse group of people has much to offer for the future of the United States.

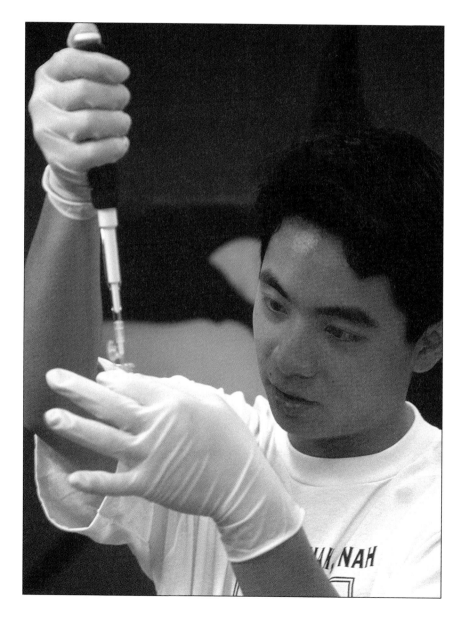

Today, many Asian-Americans make significant contributions to society in the United States.

GLOSSARY

agriculture – the business of farming or growing crops

apt – quick to learn things

blacksmith – person who makes and repairs things made of iron

dike – a high wall or dam that is built to hold back water and prevent flooding

diverse – varied or assorted

foreigner – person from another country

frontier – the far edge of a country, where few people live

immigrant – person who moves to a new country to live permanently

laborer

laborer – person who does difficult, physically exhausting work

labor union – organization that tries to get better working conditions and more money for workers

legislature – group of people responsible for making laws for a state or country

levee – a raised area bordering an irrigated field

merchant – person who buys and sells goods, a shopkeeper or trader

merchant

migrant – person who moves temporarily from one place to another in search of work

moral – honest and decent, knowing the difference between right and wrong

quota – maximum number of people that may be admitted to a country

sickle – tool with a short handle and a curved blade that is used for cutting grain, grass, or weeds

urban – relating to a city

TIMELINE

U.S. Naturalization Law restricts **1790** citizenship to white people

Twenty-five thousand Chinese go { **1848** Gold discovered at Sutter's Mill, California
to California during Gold Rush { **1852** California imposes tax of $3 per month on foreign miners

1864

Fourteenth Amendment gives **1868**
citizenship rights to former slaves **1869**

Ten thousand Chinese workers help build the transcontinental railroad

1877

Chinese Exclusion **1882**
Act prohibits
Chinese laborers
from entering the
United States

Anti-Chinese
riots break out in
San Francisco
and spread to
other California
cities

1908 Gentlemen's Agreement with Japan restricts Japanese immigration to the United States

1924 United States prohibits all Asian immigration

1952 United States removes citizenship restrictions against Asian-Americans

United States repeals immigration quotas **1965**
based on race and ethnic origin

2000 U.S. Census Bureau estimates there are ten million Asian-Americans in the United States

DEDICATION
For Eric, Nicholas, and Cameron

INDEX *(Boldface page numbers indicate illustrations.)*

PHOTO CREDITS

Photographs ©: AP/Wide World Photos: 13 bottom; Archive Photos: 12; California State Library, History Section: 11, 16, 25; Corbis-Bettmann: 17 (Hulton-Deutsch Collection), 15 (Museum of History & Industry), 29 (Jim Sugar Photography), 3, 9, 14, 18, 21 bottom, 22, 30 top, 31 top right, 31 bottom right; North Wind Picture Archives: 2, 6, 7, 8, 23; San Diego Historical Society, Photograph Collection: 1, 13 top, 20, 24, 30 bottom; Stock Montage, Inc.: cover, 4, 5, 10, 19, 21 top, 27, 31 left.

PICTURE IDENTIFICATIONS
Cover: A Chinatown grocery store in the early 1900s; Title Page: Asian-Americans working on the San Diego Flume in 1887; Page 2: A Chinatown street in San Francisco, California, in the 1880s

ABOUT THE AUTHOR
Gail Sakurai is a children's author who specializes in retelling folk tales and writing nonfiction for young readers. *Asian-Americans in the Old West* is her ninth book. Ms. Sakurai lives in Cincinnati, Ohio, with her husband and two sons. When she is not researching or writing, she enjoys traveling with her family and visiting America's historical sites.